Specific Skills

Phonemic Awareness

Practice and Play with Sounds in Spoken Words by Recognizing, Isolating, Identifying, Blending, and Manipulating Phonemes

by
Anchor R. Shepherd, Ed.S.
and
Leland Graham, Ph.D.

illustrated by
Janet Armbrust

Publisher
Key Education Publishing Company, LLC
Minneapolis, Minnesota

CONGRATULATIONS ON YOUR PURCHASE OF A KEY EDUCATION PRODUCT!

The editors at Key Education are former teachers who bring experience, enthusiasm, and quality to each and every product. Thousands of teachers have looked to the staff at Key Education for new and innovative resources to make their work more enjoyable and rewarding. We are committed to developing educational materials that will assist teachers in building a strong and developmentally appropriate curriculum for young children.

PLAN FOR GREAT TEACHING EXPERIENCES WHEN YOU USE
EDUCATIONAL MATERIALS FROM KEY EDUCATION PUBLISHING COMPANY, LLC

About the Authors

Dr. Leland Graham is a former college professor, principal, and teacher, who was twice voted "Outstanding Teacher of the Year." The author of 74 educational books, Dr. Graham is a popular speaker and workshop presenter throughout Georgia and the USA, as well as a presenter for NSSEA (National School Supply & Equipment Association). Thousands of teachers have benefited from his workshops on reading, phonics, math, and improving achievement scores."

After earning a Bachelor's Degree at Indiana University, **Anchor R. "Bunny" Shepherd** began her educational career in Fort Wayne, Indiana, with HeadStart. Following a move to Florida to teach Kindergarten, she and her family relocated to Georgia, where she continued her education at the University of West Georgia, majoring in Early Childhood and Administration & Supervision. She has been a teacher of Kindergarten-Third Grades, Infant/Toddler Evaluator, Adult Educator, administrator, and Literacy Coach. Bunny is a strong proponent of fostering literacy in young children and their teachers and is always eager to share her passion.

Acknowledgments

The authors would like to acknowledge the assistance and suggestions of the following persons: Suzanne Gleason, A. Elizabeth Hurst, Diane LaPointe, Cesar Macedo, and Charles L. Shepherd.

Credits

Authors: Anchor R. Shepherd, M.Ed.
and Leland Graham, Ph.D.
Publisher: Sherrill B. Flora
Inside Illustrations: Janet Ambrust
Editors: Debra Olson Pressnall, Karen Seberg
Cover Design: Annette Hollister-Papp
Page Design and Layout: Key Education Staff
Cover Photographs: © Comstock, © Shutterstock,
© Photo Disc, and © Able Stock

Key Education welcomes manuscripts and product ideas from teachers. For a copy of our submission guidelines, please send a self-addressed, stamped envelope to:

Key Education Publishing Company, LLC
Acquisitions Department
9601 Newton Avenue South
Minneapolis, Minnesota 55431

Copyright Notice

Standard Book Number: 978-1-602680-09-8
Specific Skills: Phonemic Awareness
Copyright © 2008 by Key Education Publishing Company, LLC
Minneapolis, Minnesota 55431

Table of Contents

Introduction

Meet the needs of various children with the Specific Skills series. Here at your fingertips is a collection of activities to foster in children an awareness of how spoken words can be broken down into the smallest units known as phonemes, or discrete sounds. The small-group lessons, hands-on activities, and easy-to-play games focus on the skills of recognizing, isolating, identifying, blending, and manipulating phonemes. In addition, this reproducible resource book offers tools for assessing each child's level of phonemic awareness.

Specific Skills: Phonemic Awareness supports the NAEYC (National Association for the Education of Young Children) and IRA (International Reading Association) position statement by providing instructional materials that sensitize children to spoken sounds, build their awareness of rhyme and phonemes, and engage them in activities and explicit lessons for more advanced skill development. According to the report issued by the National Reading Panel, the mastery of these essential phonemic awareness skills actually enables beginning readers to understand that letters in printed words have associated sounds that can also be blended and manipulated.

Dear Parent,

Over the course of the next several weeks, our class will be learning about phonemic awareness (the ability to recognize and use the individual sounds in words). We will be completing activity sheets and participating in hands-on, fun activities to help better understand phonemic concepts.

You may see some of the activity sheets in your child's homework folder. Review the work with him/her. Note the accomplishments and/or the problems he/she may be having with phonemes (the smallest part of sound in a spoken word). As you share a bedtime story with your child each night, encourage and assist him/her in listening for the different phonemes. Discuss the placement of phonemes in words.

Please help your child maintain a good attitude and self-confidence about phonemic awareness. This will promote an eagerness to read as well as the knowledge that we are all working together to achieve success!

Thank you so much for your time and assistance.

Sincerely,

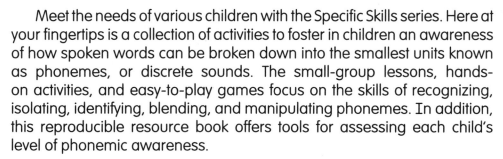

Specific Skills Phonemic Awareness Assessment

Student's Name:_____

Assessed by:_____

1st Assessment Date: _____

2nd Assessment Date: _____

3rd Assessment Date: _____

The Specific Skills Phonemic Awareness Assessment is designed to be used as an informal assessment tool to assist teachers in determining each student's understanding of phonemic awareness, including specific skills that have been mastered and skills that are not as yet understood. The following assessment can be used as a pre-test, postest, and to provide documentation of the progress of each stuident.

The Specific Skills Phonemic Awareness Assessment is an oral assessment. Reproduce pages 5 and 6 for each student and record the student's reponses as you administer the assessment. If you see that the child is struggling and misses more than 3 questions in a section, skip the remaining part of that section and move to the next. Mark each box according to the student's reponse.

1. Rhyming Words

Listen carefully. I am going to say two words: *cat* and *mat*. These words rhyme because they have the same ending sound. The words *cat* and *mouse* do not rhyme. *(Model more examples if the student looks unsure.)* I am going to say some more words. You can say "yes" if you think the words rhyme or "no" if you do not think the words rhyme.

a. **dog – hog** ❑ correct ❑ incorrect
b. **sun – fun** ❑ correct ❑ incorrect
c. **dog – frog** ❑ correct ❑ incorrect
d. **map – cot** ❑ correct ❑ incorrect

e. **mice – nice** ❑ correct ❑ incorrect
f. **cow – can** ❑ correct ❑ incorrect
g. **pan – ran** ❑ correct ❑ incorrect
h. **look – book** ❑ correct ❑ incorrect

Subtotal ❑ correct ❑ incorrect

2. Matching Beginning Phonemes

Listen carefully. I am going to say three words: *boy, baby,* and *bat*. These words all begin with the same some sound /b/. *(Model more examples if the student looks unsure.)* Now, I will say three more words— two of the words have the same beginning sound. You are to tell me which two words begin with the same sound..

a. **bike – face – bear** ❑ correct ❑ incorrect
b. **duck – deer – goat** ❑ correct ❑ incorrect
c. **gum – fan – foot** ❑ correct ❑ incorrect

d. **jacks – leaf – jump** ❑ correct ❑ incorrect
e. **top – moon – me** ❑ correct ❑ incorrect
f. **pear – pie – house** ❑ correct ❑ incorrect

Subtotal ❑ correct ❑ incorrect

3. Isolating Beginning Phonemes

Listen carefully. I am going to say a word. I would like you to tell me the first sound of the word. If I said, "*top*," you would say /t/. *(Model more examples if the student looks unsure.)* Repeat each word and then say the first sound.

a. **kite /k/** ❑ correct ❑ incorrect
b. **bike /b/** ❑ correct ❑ incorrect
c. **house /h/** ❑ correct ❑ incorrect
d. **rose /r/** ❑ correct ❑ incorrect

e. **man /m/** ❑ correct ❑ incorrect
f. **doll /d/** ❑ correct ❑ incorrect
g. **seal /s/** ❑ correct ❑ incorrect
h. **lamp /l/** ❑ correct ❑ incorrect

Subtotal ❑ correct ❑ incorrect

4. Matching Final Phonemes

Listen carefully. I am going to say three words: *tent, bat,* and *foot*. These words all have the same ending sound /t/. *(Model more examples if the student looks unsure.)* Now, I will say three more words— two of the words have the same ending sound. You are to tell me which two words end with the same sound..

a. **web – tub – can** ❑ correct ❑ incorrect
b. **bug – frog – cat** ❑ correct ❑ incorrect
c. **drum – pig – worm** ❑ correct ❑ incorrect

d. **mop – hen – can** ❑ correct ❑ incorrect
e. **net – five – coat** ❑ correct ❑ incorrect
f. **top – sheep – bird** ❑ correct ❑ incorrect

Subtotal ❑ correct ❑ incorrect

5. Isolating Final Phonemes

Listen carefully. I am going to say a word. I would like you to tell me the ending sound of the word. If I said, "*dog,*" you would say /g/. *(Model more examples if the student looks unsure.)* Repeat each word and then say the last sound.

a. crab /b/ ❑ correct ❑ incorrect   e. pail /l/ ❑ correct ❑ incorrect
b. bird /d/ ❑ correct ❑ incorrect   f. ran /n/ ❑ correct ❑ incorrect
c. rug /g/ ❑ correct ❑ incorrect   g. broom /m/ ❑ correct ❑ incorrect
d. clock /k/ ❑ correct ❑ incorrect   h. boat /t/ ❑ correct ❑ incorrect

Subtotal ❑ correct ❑ incorrect

6. Blending Phonemes

Listen carefully. I am going to say some sounds and you are going to put the sounds together to make a word. For example, if I say /b/ /i/ /g/, the word would be *big*. *(Model more examples if the student looks unsure.)* Are you ready? I will say the sounds and then you say the word.

a. run ❑ correct ❑ incorrect   e. sock ❑ correct ❑ incorrect
b. sit ❑ correct ❑ incorrect   f. ball ❑ correct ❑ incorrect
c. fan ❑ correct ❑ incorrect   g. hand ❑ correct ❑ incorrect
d. dish ❑ correct ❑ incorrect   h. jump ❑ correct ❑ incorrect

Subtotal ❑ correct ❑ incorrect

7. Segmenting Phonemes

Listen carefully. This time I am going to say a word and you are going to break the word apart. For example, if I say *dog*, you would say /d/ /o/ /g/. *(Model more examples if the student looks unsure.)* Are you ready? I will say the words and then you say the sounds.

a. /c/ /a/ /t/ ❑ correct ❑ incorrect   e. /ch/ /i/ /p/ ❑ correct ❑ incorrect
b. /f/ /i/ /sh/ ❑ correct ❑ incorrect   f. /t/ /u/ /b/ ❑ correct ❑ incorrect
c. /m/ /a/ /n/ ❑ correct ❑ incorrect   g. /b/ /e/ /ll/ ❑ correct ❑ incorrect
d. /r/ /e/ /d/ ❑ correct ❑ incorrect   h. /s/ /o/ /ck/ ❑ correct ❑ incorrect

Subtotal ❑ correct ❑ incorrect

8. Recognizing Syllables

Listen carefully. I am going to say a word, clap my hands, and count each syllable—demonstrate *cupcake*, with two caps, and then say "two." *(Model more examples if the student looks unsure.)* Are you ready? I will say a word and then you repeat the word, clap, and count how many syllables are in the word.

a. fish ❑ correct ❑ incorrect   e. but – ter – fly ❑ correct ❑ incorrect
b. desk ❑ correct ❑ incorrect   f. mon – key ❑ correct ❑ incorrect
c. ta – ble ❑ correct ❑ incorrect   g. di – no – saur ❑ correct ❑ incorrect
d. ro – bin ❑ correct ❑ incorrect   h. pup – py ❑ correct ❑ incorrect

Subtotal ❑ correct ❑ incorrect

9. Manipulating Phonemes

(This is by far the most difficult section because it deals with skills that are not usually mastered until after kindergarten.) Listen carefully. I am going to say a word and then ask you to make a new word. For example, if I said, "*rain*" and asked you to add a /t/, you would say "*train.*" If I said, "*blast*" and asked you to take way the /b/, you would say "*last.*" If I said "*cot*" and asked you to change the /c/ to /d/, you would say "*dot.*" *(Model more examples if the student looks unsure.)* .

a. lap, add an /c/ (clap) ❑ correct ❑ incorrect   e. candy, take away /k/ (Andy) ❑ correct ❑ incorrect
b. ear, add a /t/ (tear) ❑ correct ❑ incorrect   f. hat, change the /h/ to /s/ (sat) ❑ correct ❑ incorrect
c. lock, add a /k/ (clock) ❑ correct ❑ incorrect   g. lake, change the /l/ to /r/ (rake) ❑ correct ❑ incorrect
d. skid, take away /s/ (kid) ❑ correct ❑ incorrect   h. hen, change the /h/ to /p/ (pen) ❑ correct ❑ incorrect

Subtotal ❑ correct ❑ incorrect

Total for Assessment ❑ correct ❑ incorrect

Building Awareness of Sounds

While young children are busy exploring and discovering different things to make sense of their world, they need opportunities to identify and locate sounds that occur in the natural world, classroom, playground, home, and in the community. As children become more observant of various sounds, their heightened awareness of how environmental sounds differ also helps them discern and learn to identify speech sounds in oral language. Throughout the school day, there will be many learning opportunities for children to talk about sounds that are generated in the classroom or noises that happen outside the building. Be sure to help children recall the sounds they have heard during group time, transition time, rest time, snack time, and on walks in the neighborhood. The activities in this book also target alertness, discrimination, and memory skills.

Where's the Noisemaker?

Every preschooler enjoys being a noisemaker, especially when playing with blocks, trucks, balls, and musical instruments. During group time, distribute two or three common objects and/or musical instruments to each child while the children sit on the floor in a circle. Allow the group a few minutes to explore what sounds they can make with their materials. Then, direct the children to arrange their noisemakers on the floor in a special way. (This helps the children to "turn off" the noisemakers.) Begin the activity by asking children to make very soft sounds and then ask them to make sounds that are louder. Talk about the materials they used to make the sounds and what they did to change the dynamics. Continue the activity by choosing a child to be a noisemaker. Direct the remaining children to cover their eyes and listen carefully for a sound that will be made by the chosen child. The noisemaker then selects one of the instruments, walks to another part of the classroom, and makes a soft sound behind a large object. Have the children uncover their eyes. Ask: "Where is the noisemaker?" and "What did the noisemaker use to make the noise?" Continue as time and interest allow.

Magic Box Sounds!

Many animals can be identified by the sounds they make to communicate. To prepare for this activity, copy the pictures of animals on page 9 onto colorful card stock and then cut out the picture cards. Also, make an enlargement of this page onto card stock and cut out those cards, too. Gather 12 identical boxes with covers or clean, plastic margarine tubs with lids. (Cover the containers with paper if they are not identical.) Tape each small picture to the inside bottom of a separate container. Arrange the enlarged animal cards on the tray below the chalkboard or white board. During group time, talk about the animals featured on the large cards and have children practice making the sounds that correspond with the pictures. Then, choose three children to stand in front of the group and give each one a container. Ask them to open their boxes/tubs, look inside, and then make the

corresponding animal noise (just like magic!). When finished, ask the remaining children to tell you which animal sound they heard first, next, and last. Continue in this manner by choosing three other children to make the magic box sounds.

Alternatively, read a favorite picture book about farm animals. Select some large picture cards that correspond with the text and then distribute them to the children. When the selected animals are mentioned as you read aloud the story, the children holding the cards can generate the sound effects for those animals. If interested, you will find that the pictures on page 9 actually correspond with the animals featured in the book *The Cow Who Clucked* by Denise Fleming (Henry Holt, 2006). This delightful story is about a cow that must listen carefully to the other animals to find out which one is making the wrong sound.

What Did You Hear?

For this activity, copy page 10 onto colorful card stock and then cut out the cards. Gather the necessary materials—such as scissors and tagboard, dried split peas or rice to make a shaker, marbles and a plastic container with lid, and so on—to make the corresponding sounds indicated by the pictures. Place the prepared materials behind a large box or something else to keep them hidden from children. During group time, ask children to sit in front of the box. Without letting them watch you, make a sound depicted by one of the picture cards and then ask children to explain how the sound was made and pick out the matching card. Continue this activity by making other sounds.

Alternatively, choose a child to be the noisemaker. Have the child stand behind the box, draw two picture cards from a pile, and then make the corresponding sounds. When finished, ask the group of children: "What sound did you hear first? last?" Continue in this manner by choosing other children to be noisemakers. If the group is ready for more challenging listening experiences, have the noisemaker make three different sounds.

(Directions are found on page 8.)

Magic Box Sounds! Cards

Pictures: cow, dog, bumblebee, cat, fish, duck, goat, mouse, snake, squirrel, owl, hen

 Specific Skills: Phonemic Awareness

(Directions are found on page 8.)

What Did You Hear? Cards

Pictures: clapping hands, ringing a bell, crumpling paper, dropping a book, tapping rhythm sticks, shaking a jar of marbles, shaking a container of rice, tearing paper, popping bubbles in packaging wrap, cutting poster board, zipping up a zipper, saying "Shhhhhh"

Building Awareness of Rhymes

In the last 10 to 20 years, educators have noted the decline of the recognition of nursery rhymes on the part of their young students. At this time the reasons for this phenomenon will not be analyzed, and instead we'll simply focus on the importance of having young children—infant to five year olds—hear rhyming words via nursery rhymes, poetry, picture books, nonsense words, finger plays, and so on.

The awareness and recognition of rhyming words is a necessary step in learning to read. As young children begin to become cognizant of the predictable language in books, such as *Brown Bear, Brown Bear, What Do You See?* by Bill Martin Jr. and illustrated by Eric Carle (Henry Holt and Company, 1992), they also begin to notice that certain words rhyme. For example: "Brown bear, brown bear, what do you *see*? I see a red bird looking at *me*." As children listen to the remainder of the book, and the teacher emphasizes the rhyming words, the awareness of rhyme becomes sharper. Foster this skill by selecting text that feature common phonograms because the next step for emerging readers is to make the connection that some rhyming words end with the same letters.

Picture books with rhyming texts are a wonderful way to engage young children with word play. As children become attuned to onset and rimes (initial consonant sounds and word endings that include the vowel sounds), they are also able to create nonsense words. This manipulation of sounds is an important skill because children are applying their knowledge of letter sounds to create the nonsense words. Teachers and parents need not be concerned with the spelling of nonsense words, since by their very name "nonsense words," there will not be correct spellings.

The following activities will aid teachers in teaching the awareness of rhyme. Tailor the activities to meet the needs of children. Throughout the day, weave into your curriculum engaging word play. Whether it is making up silly rhymes with children's names and common objects, or chanting a favorite nursery rhyme during transition time and having children listen for a certain word as the cue to move to another part of the room, make the experiences fun!

Mother Goose on the Loose

Locate a few picture books on Mother Goose Nursery Rhymes and place them in your reading corner. Choose a few rhymes that you plan on chanting during the day and mark those pages with large colorful bookmarks for those children who may be interested in "reading" them independently.

Incorporate opportunities for chanting and acting out nursery rhymes. During snack time, transition time, or group time, children can chant a selected rhyme and clap on the rhyming words. To build awareness of words, you may wish to ask children how many words they hear in a certain phrase or to tell you which words rhyme. Perhaps the children would like to "act out" the rhyme using a few props and have an audience recite the rhyme with them. The following rhyme is fun for young children to dramatize:

Little Miss Muffet
Sat on a tuffet,
Eating her curds and whey.
Along came a spider
Who sat down beside her.
And frightened Miss Muffet away.

Playing with Real and Nonsense Words

Using the rhyme "Little Miss Muffet," replace "Miss Muffet's" name with a student's name and use nonsense words that rhyme. Then, have the class recite the rhyme. Any time a child's name can be used in a rhyme, the more involved and eager the children will be to participate. It's fun to put yourself in a rhyme! Here are two examples:

Little Miss *Alisha*
Sat on a *risha,*
Eating her curds and *rice.*
Along came a spider
Who sat down beside her
And frightened Miss *Alisha apice.*

Little *Mr. Bobby*
Sat on a *mobby,*
Eating his curds and *flakes.*
Along came a spider
Who sat down beside *him*
And frightened *Mr. Bobby adakes.*

Familiar finger plays can also be used when working with actual and nonsense words that rhyme! Here is a humorous version based on the "Eensy, Weensy Spider" that children can illustrate, too. Of course, challenge children to think of other animals and different outcomes to change the rhyme.

The eensy, weensy gorilla
Climbed up a great big *tree.*
Down came the hail
And covered up one *knee.*

Out came the sun
To melt all the *hail*
And the eensy, weensy gorilla
Really began to *wail.*

Read–Aloud Books with Rhyming Text

No doubt, there are colorful picture books with delightful rhyming words on your bookshelf. This treasure of wonderful word play can be an effective tool to help children discriminate the subtleties in letter sounds. Only after your children are familiar with a book, then draw their attention to words that rhyme or have them fill in the story line by calling out rhyming words for chosen phrases. Here are a few picture books that children may enjoy hearing:

- *Snuggle Wuggle* by Jonathan London and illustrated by Michael Rex (Harcourt, 2000). To help young preschoolers notice rhyming words, this picture book has simple rhyming text. In this selection, young readers are introduced to twelve different animals that hug in different ways. For example: "How does a bunny hug? Snuggle wuggle, snuggle wuggle." The large text and colorful illustrations make it easy for a small group of children to view the pages. Some observant children may notice that all of the featured animals are included in the final scene.

- *Smash! Mash! Crash! There Goes the Trash!* by Barbara Odanaka and illustrated by Will Hillenbrand (Margaret K. McElderry Books, 2006). This rhythmic text will engage the minds of active prereaders! Be sure to let children enjoy the story and illustrations before "chomping" on rhyming words.

- *Do You Have a Hat?* by Eileen Spinelli and illustrated by Geraldo Valério (Simon & Schuster, 2004). Whether you are planning on hosting a "Hat Day" or not, this picture book may be of interest to students in preschool, kindergarten, or first grade. Children will be fascinated by the featured people and their hats, such as Amelia Earhart (well-known aviator).

Name _____   Date _____

Recognizing Words in Sentences and Identifying Rhyming Words

The cat sat on the hat. The fat rat sat on the bat.

To the Teacher: Before showing the page to the children, read the sentence aloud several times. Ask children to count the words that they hear in the sentence. Talk about words that rhyme with *cat.* Have the children look at the picture and offer other rhyming words.

The hen needs ten pens.

To the Teacher: Before showing the page to the children, read the sentence aloud several times. Ask children to count the words that they hear in the sentence. Talk about words that rhyme with *hen.* Have the children look at the picture and offer other rhyming words.

Recognizing Words in Sentences and Identifying Rhyming Words

Do you think the chick will kick the thick stick?

The boy said, "Let's have fun and run in the sun."

Picture Rhyme Game

Picture Rhyme Game Cards

Copy the Picture Rhyme game cards below and the Picture Rhyme game boards found on pages 16 and 17. The game cards should be placed face down. Have the children take turns drawing cards. A player keeps the picture game card and places it on their game board if the picture on the card rhymes with a picture on their game board. If there is not a matching rhyme the card is placed at the bottom of the card pile.

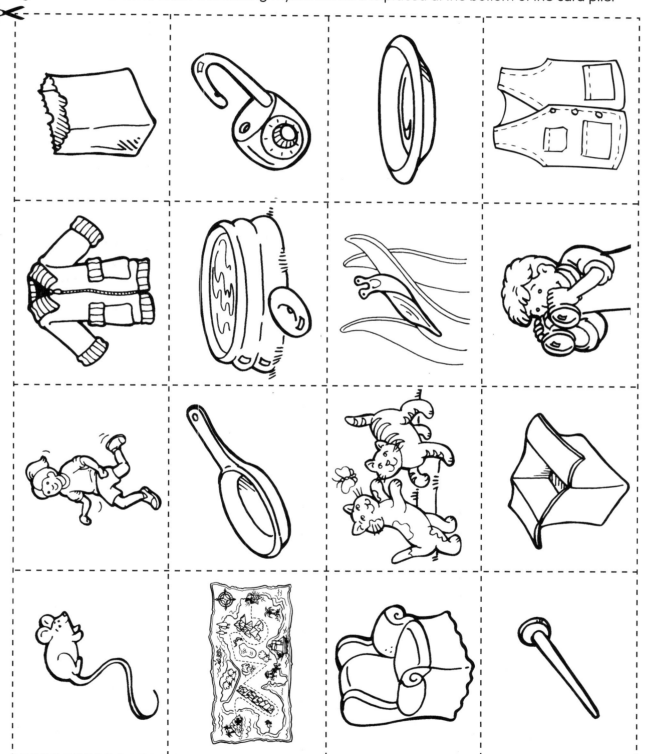

Row 1: mouse, run, coat, bag - Row 2: map, pan, pool, lock Row 3: chair, kittens, slug, dish - Row 4: nail, box, see, vest

Picture Rhyme Game Board

Picture Rhyme Game Board

Picture Rhyme Game Board

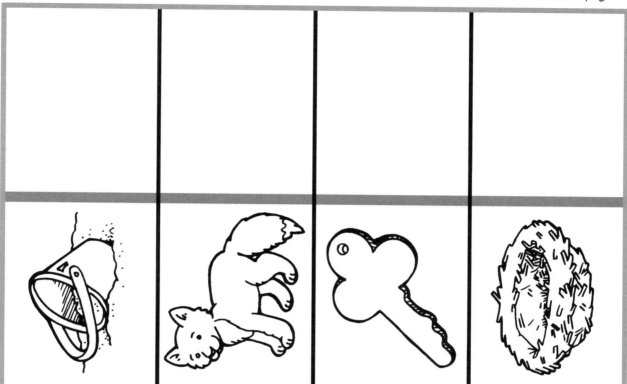

Picture Rhyme Game Board

17 *Specific Skills: Phonemic Awareness*

Identifying Rhyming Words

(Building Awareness of Rhymes)

To the Teacher: Reproduce this page for each student. Read the names of the pictures aloud. Have the children circle the two pictures in each row whose names rhyme. The following pictures are shown: Row 1: goat, grape, boat; Row 2: car, star, bird; Row 3: bat, drum, hat; Row 4: snake, rope, cake.

Saying Word Parts: After reviewing the names of the pictures, direct the children to separate each word into two parts (initial consonant sound and rime) and say the sounds. For example, *goat* would be /g/ and /oat/.

More Identifying Rhyming Words

(Building Awareness of Rhymes)

To the Teacher: Reproduce this page for each student. Read the names of the pictures aloud. Have the children circle the two pictures in each row whose names rhyme. The following pictures are shown: Row 1: bridge, dish, fish; Row 2: gate, skate, bee; Row 3: baby, sunny, money; Row 4: kitten, button, mitten; Row 5: grape, cape, cane.

Something Else to Try: Repeat the names of the pictures randomly by separating them into two sounds, the initial consonant sound and the rime. Say, "What is the mystery word for [pronounce /g/ (pause) /ate/]?" Have the children point to the corresponding picture and say the word *gate* correctly.

Does It Rhyme? Game

To the Teacher: Copy the two faces below onto card stock, making a set of cards for each child. Cut out the cards along the dashed lines. Distribute one set along with two craft sticks to each child. Have children glue their cards to their craft sticks to make small props. Read aloud each of the following sentences. Direct children to hold up the appropriate card: the smiley face if two or more words rhyme in the sentence or the sad face if no rhyming words are heard. Alternatively, use sentences and phrases from Mother Goose rhymes and favorite children's picture books when playing the game.

1. Let's bounce the **ball** on the **wall**.

2. The little boy went to school.

3. The big **pot** is very **hot**.

4. Are you mad at your brother?

5. The **rain** hit the window **pane**.

6. Look at the box full of toys.

7. I like **potatoes** and **tomatoes**.

8. The green **frog** sat on the brown **log**.

9. The black **cat sat** on the red **hat**.

10. The girl didn't like the buttons on her coat.

11. My mother says, "**Bill** is **ill**!"

12. The teacher asked if we were done.

13. The big **tank** crashed through the **bank**.

14. Help! Help! The **tire** is on **fire**.

15. The tractor hit a big bump.

16. I have a lot of holes in my socks.

17. I asked my dad to **look** at my **book**.

18. The ferris wheel and the merry-go-round are my favorite rides.

19. Do you think **mice** are **nice**?

20. Watch the **fox** push that **box**!

Building Awareness of Alliteration

When children have a breakthrough and start to recognize a string of words in stories that begin with the same initial phoneme, you know that they are using their listening skills to detect finer differences in sounds. Many picture books and nursery rhymes feature names or groupings of two or more words in sentences that begin with the same sounds. This literary element is called *alliteration*.

It is very easy to include some experiences with alliteration in the curriculum by choosing rhymes for children to hear and recite during small-group time and snack time. To make a listening activity fun during transition time, choose an alliterative name or phrase and change the wording of the rhyme if necessary. Then, direct children to stop and listen for your "magic word(s)" while you recite the rhyme. When they hear the "magic word(s)" they can then move to the new location.

Mother Goose Rhymes Having Alliteration

- Little Tommy Tittlemouse lived in a little house. . . .
- Daffy-Down-Dilly has now come to town . . .
- Diddlety, diddlety, dumpty, the cat ran up the plum tree. . . .
- Peter Piper picked a peck of pickled peppers. . . .
- Lucy Locket lost her pocket, Kitty Fisher found it. . . .
- Diddle diddle dumpling, my son John went to bed with his clothes on. . . .
- Pease porridge hot, pease porridge cold, . . .
- Sing a song of sixpence, a pocket full of rye; . . .
- Wee Willie Winkie runs through the town, . . .
- Fiddle-de-dee, fiddle-de-dee, the fly shall marry the bumblebee. . . .
- Simple Simon met a pie man going to the fair. . . .

Read–Aloud Books with Alliteration

Here are two picture books that children in your classroom may enjoy hearing:

- *Jiggle Joggle Jee!* by Laura E. Richards and illustrated by Sam Williams (Greenwillow Books, 2001). This picture book features a poem written by Laura Richards in the early 1900s that was intended for family members to chant while bouncing babies and toddlers on their laps. Perhaps young preschoolers would enjoy hearing the poem as part of a lesson on recognizing alliteration—"jiggle joggle, jiggle, joggle, jee"—or rhyme—"lokey mokey poky stoky smoky choky chee." Encourage children to experiment by substituting other initial sounds when repeating the familiar phrase: "diggle doggle, diggle doggle, dee" ; miggle moggle, miggle moggle, mee"; and so on when reading the story.

- *Chicky Chicky Chook Chook* by Cathy MacLennan (Boxer Books, 2007). Chicks, busy bees, and kitty cats play and sleep in the warm sunshine until it rains, after which their "f-f-fluff and f-f-fur and f-f-fuzz" must dry. There is lots of engaging use of language for prereaders in this book!

(Building Awareness of Alliteration)

Recognizing Words in Sentences and Beginning Sounds: /f/ and /d/

Are there four or five funny fish?

Which animals bark — a dozen dogs or a dozen ducks?

Name _____ Date _____

Recognizing Words in Sentences and Beginning Sounds: /p/ and /r/

Do you like peas in a pod or a pear in a pot?

To the Teacher: Before showing the page to the children, read the sentence aloud. Ask children to count the words in the sentence. Then, talk about the sound /p/ that is heard at the beginning of four words. Have the children answer the question while looking at the picture.

Do you see the round, ruby ring on the rug or the rocks?

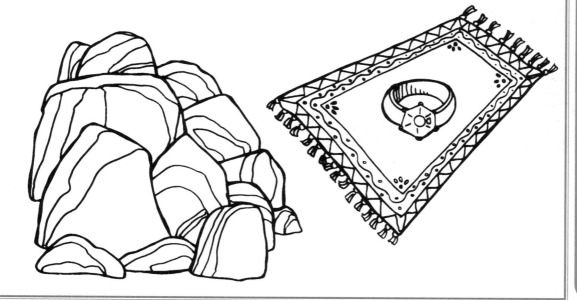

To the Teacher: Before showing the page to the children, read the sentence aloud. Ask children to count the words in the sentence. Then, talk about the sound /r/ that is heard at the beginning of five words. Have the children answer the question while looking at the picture.

Isolating Sounds

Phonemes are the smallest units of sound in a word, which are represented by individual letters or letter clusters, not phonograms. The next logical instructional step after children demonstrate proficiency in identifying rhyming words is to help them discover these small units of sound. How is this possible? Begin the process by having children analyze words with the CVC structure (consonant-vowel-consonant pattern). Choose a CVC word and then say it out loud to the children. If possible, prolong or stretch out the initial consonant sound, such as *man*—/mmmmman/. Ask students to tell you the beginning sound in the word. Continue in the same manner with other chosen words. When children can recognize, isolate, and pronounce beginning consonant sounds, build on this skill by talking about and identifying the final sounds in simple words.

Note: Continuant consonant sounds are easier to hear and isolate in words than those sounds that abruptly stop. Continuant sounds include /h/, /f/, /l/, /m/, /n/, /r/, /s/, /v/, /z/, /ch/, and /th/.

Cool and Creamy Word Parts

Give each child a copy of the Cool and Creamy Word Parts Patterns on page 25. Have children color their "ice cream" scoops to make them represent two different "flavors" and then cut out the pieces. Set aside one of the ice cream scoops. Explain how a scoop of ice cream will stand for the beginning sound of a word and the cone will hold the remaining word part (rime). For example, say, "Let's build a cool and creamy word treat for the word *ran*." Pronounce the word again by stretching the first sound—/rrrrrrr/ -*an*. Point to the "scoop of ice cream" and say the /rrrrrrr/ sound. Next, point to the "cone" and say /an/. Finally, repeat the entire word quickly — /ran/. Tell children: "Now say the first sound in *ran* with me—/rrrrrrr/." Have children tell you again the beginning sound of the word. Continue the activity by making additional cool and creamy word treats with other words. Each time, direct children to change the flavor of the cone for a new word. Some examples of words include the following: *man, tan*, and *van*; *mad, sad*, and *fad*; *bat, cat, hat*, and *mat*; *bell, fell, jell*, and *sell*; *jet, met, net*, and *wet*; *dim, him*, and *rim*; *lip, rip*, and *zip*; *dish, fish*, and *wish*; and *bug, dug, hug, jug, mug*, and *rug*.

Building Word Rigs

Make a copy of the Building Word Rigs Patterns on page 26 for each child. Have children color their semi trucks' tractors and trailers and then cut out the pieces. After each child's pieces are arranged to show the rig, explain how the semi's tractor will stand for the first sound in a word, the middle piece will stand for the middle sound, and the end trailer will stand for the final sound in a word. Ask various questions about words. For example: "Where is the /f/ sound in *fish*?" Say the word again, sound by sound, /f/-/i/-/sh/. (Beginning) "Where is the /n/ sound in *ten, /t/-/e/-/n/*?" (End) "Where is the /a/ sound in *bat, /b/-/a/-/t/*?" (Middle) Continue asking questions about CVC words while children answer you by pointing to the corresponding part of their "Word Rigs."

Alternatively, announce that the Word Rigs will be hauling tasty snacks. Give each child three paper cups, one for each section of the truck, and a small bowl of cereal pieces and/or dried fruit. Each time you ask a question about a word, the child places a snack piece in the corresponding cup. At the end of the activity, invite children to snack on the "cargo."

(Directions are found on page 24.)

Cool and Creamy Word Parts
Patterns

25

(Directions are found on page 24.)

26

Matching Phonemes

After children have learned how to isolate initial and final phonemes in words, they will then be ready to identify other words that either begin or end with the same sounds. The following activities will focus on matching sounds word to word. A great resource of words that begin with the same letter is the collection of ABC books on your book shelf.

I Spy Things for Sounds

For a fun and easy way to introduce the concept of matching initial phonemes, collect various common materials whose names begin with the same sound. Locate two or three objects for each sound: /d/, /f/, /l/, /m/, and /t/. Place the collected materials in the center of the playing area. Be sure to add a few objects to the collection that do not fit the criteria. Have children sit in a circle around the objects. Say: "I spy something that starts with the sound /m/? "The children could point and say [e.g, monkey, mouse, marbles, magnets]. Continue the game as time and interest allow. Other groups of objects can be collected for sounds: /h/, /k/, /n/, /p/, /s/, /b/, hard /g/, /v/, /y/, or /z/.

Let's Tell a Story!

Play the "I Spy" game again as directed above. At the end of each round, choose children to hold the chosen objects. Continue in the same manner until everyone has been given an object. Then, invite the children to work in teams and make up an alliterative story (two or three sentences) about those objects. As the children create their stories, that can be silly, also remind them to include as many other words that start with the assigned sound. Encourage them to look at ABC picture books for ideas. When the project is finished, have students tell and act out their stories to the rest of the class.

Whose Name Begins with . . .?

Here is another twist on the "I Spy" game. This time ask questions that relate to the names of children in your classroom. If more than one child's name starts with the same sound, ask the question "I am thinking about someone whose name begins with [make the sound]. Who is this person?" The children may have to offer more than one answer before guessing the correct name. Alternatively, drop the initial phoneme and then say the name of the child. Invite the class to tell whose name you meant to say. For example, say, "I spy someone in the room whose name ends like _ayla. Who is this person?" (Kayla)

Sorting Sounds

Reproduce the Sorting Sounds Cards found on pages 28–33 and the Sorting Board found on page 34. The children can sort the cards according to initial phonemes /b/, /d/, /f/, /g/, /h/, /j/, /k/, /l/, /m/, /n/, /p/, /r/, /s/, /t/, /v/, /w/, /z/; digraphs /ch/, /sh/, /th/, /wh/; and rows 22-24 (page 33) are included so pictures can be sorted by vowel sounds. Have the children place the matching cards in one section of the Sorting Board.

Say and Match Sounds

To play this game, copy the game board patterns on pages 35–36 and the Sorting Sounds Cards on pages 28–33. Color and laminate for durability. Provide two or three game markers along with a standard die. To play the game, the players will take turns drawing cards, isolating the initial phoneme in the name of the picture and saying it out loud. If correct, the child rolls the die and moves their game marker the corresponding number of spaces on the path. If a "6" is rolled, the player rolls the die again.

Pictures: Row I: bed, bear, bike; Row 2: duck, deer, desk;
Row 3: feather, football, face; Row 4: goat, gum, gate

Sorting Sounds Cards
(Directions are found on page 27.)

Pictures: Row 5: hammer, hair, hose; Row 6: jacks, jump, jay;
Row 7: king, kite, kangaroo; Row 8: ladder, leaf, lips

Sorting Sounds Cards
(Directions are found on page 27.)

Pictures: Row 9: mice, marbles, mask; Row 10: nose, nest, nail;
Row 11: pear, pie, puppet; Row 12: rose, rattle, ring

Sorting Sounds Cards
(Directions are found on page 27.)

Pictures: Row 13: seal, sailboat, seeds; Row 14: tail, top, tape;
Row 15: violin, valentine, van; Row 16: wagon, web, watch

Sorting Sounds Cards
(Directions are found on page 27.)

Pictures: Row 17: zipper, zebra, zero; Row 18: chick, chest, cherries;
Row 19: shark, sheep, shoes; Row 20: thread, think/thirty,
thirty-three

Specific Skills: Phonemic Awareness

Pictures: Row 21: whale, wheelbarrow, wheelchair;
Row 22: clock, drum, stop;
Row 23: glue, lock, coat;
Row 24: rope, mule, ice

Sorting Board

(Directions are found on page 27.)

**Say and Match Sounds
Game Board**

Start

35 *Specific Skills: Phonemic Awareness*

Say and Match Sounds Game Board

Finish

36

Categorizing Phonemes

After children have learned how to match pairs of words by initial or final sounds, challenge them with sorting tasks. To reinforce this skill, call out three or four words for children to analyze and have them tell you which one does not belong in the group. For example, the words could be *top*, *Tom*, *bun*, and *touch*. The odd word is *bun*. A good source of words would be ABC books.

Picking a Peck of Picture Words

Chant the rhyme "Peter Piper picked a peck of pickled peppers" with the children. (If needed, the entire tongue twister can be found in *Sylvia Long's Mother Goose* (Chronicle Books, 1999.) Have children call out words that begin with the /p/ sound. Continue the lesson by chanting the rhyme "Peter, Peter, Pumpkin Eater." This rhyme is also printed in Sylvia Long's book along with her delightful illustration that shows the wife being very comfortable in her pumpkin house. Finally, have children generate words that begin with the /b/ sound after chanting the rhyme "Baa, Baa, Black Sheep." The class may also enjoy reciting the rhyme "Little Bo Peep" and talk about the /b/ and /p/ sounds in the title.

To prepare for the work-station activity, gather three small baskets along with three index cards. Draw one of the following on each card: a large orange pumpkin, a baseball bat, and a trash can. Give each child three cards for them to draw pictures. Have each child draw three pictures: a picture whose name begins with the /p/ sound, a picture that begins with the /b/ sound, and something else that will not belong in either category, but instead will be "dropped" into the trash can. When everyone is finished, place the materials in the center and then explain to children how they will sort all of the prepared picture-words into groups. Alternatively, choose other phonemes and corresponding nursery rhymes and have children draw correlating pictures that can be sorted.

Odd One Out!

Select words that either begin or end with the same phoneme. Say the words to a small group of children. Have them listen to the words carefully the first time. Ask: "Which word has a different [beginning or ending] sound?" Repeat the words. When they hear the word that doesn't belong, have children make the signal for "out" by raising their hands and pointing with their thumbs just like a baseball umpire.

Blending Phonemes

After children have learned to identify and isolate initial and final consonant sounds, challenge their thought processes by saying words in a segmented manner. For example, if you say /k/-/u/-/b/, have children repeat the sounds quickly until the word cub can be heard. Tailor the lessons by determining how many phonemes the children will blend. For those children in kindergarten, select words that have either two or three phonemes. Older students are capable of handling words up to four phonemes if blends and digraphs have been introduced.

Blending Sounds with Busy Buzzy Bee

Busy Buzzy Bee likes to help children learn how to blend sounds. Copy the pictures on page 43 onto colorful card stock and cut them out. Make the Busy Buzzy Bee finger puppet by following the directions on page 40. Work with a small group of children. Select two or three pictures and arrange them on a flat surface in front of the children. Say, "Busy Buzzy Bee wants one of these pictures. Listen carefully to what I say, /c/-/a/-/p/. Which picture does Busy Buzzy Bee want?" Repeat the activity in the same manner with a different picture. Continue in this manner with other picture cards as time and interest allow.

Sound It Out Kids

This is an effective lesson that demonstrates how to blend individual phonemes in words. Create a list of words that use only two or three phonemes. Then, ask three children to stand in front of the rest of the class. Choose one of the words and say each of the phonemes slowly. Ask the first child to repeat the first phoneme. Ask the second child to repeat the second phoneme and then ask the third child to repeat the third phoneme. Finally, have the children hold hands and repeat their phonemes faster this time. Ask the rest of the class if anyone in the class can identify the word.

Variation: Make multiple copies of the "kids" found on page 39. The children can color, cut out, and print an alphabet letter on each t-shirt. The "kids" can then be taped on craft sticks and used as stick puppets. The children can use the puppets to make words and blend phonemes.

Say It Slowly, Say It Fast!

This fun activity can help children learn how to blend phonemes. Copy the turtle and the rabbit puppet patterns found on page 40. The children can color, cut out, and turn them into finger puppets or tape onto craft sticks and use them as stick puppets.

Fill a box or bag with small toys or classroom objects. Pick an object out of the bag and say it just like the turtle would—very slowly. Then, have the children repeat the word back to you just like the rabbit would—very fast. Repeat in reverse. The teacher says the word quickly and the children respond slowly.

(Directions for "Sound It Out Kids" are found on page 38. Directions for "Team It Up with Sound It Out Kids" are found on page 41.)

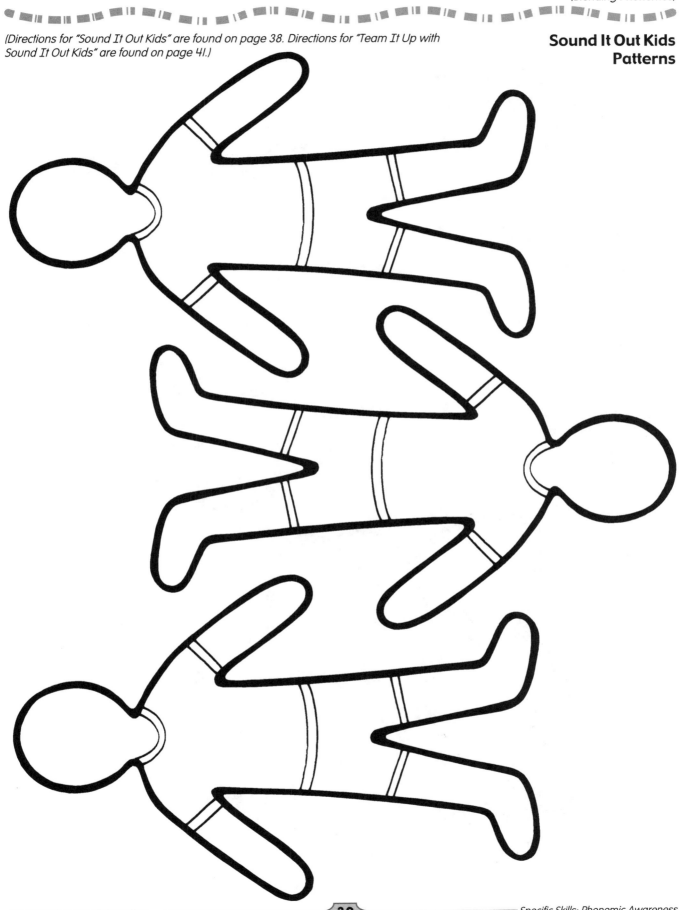

39

Specific Skills: Phonemic Awareness

(Directions are found on page 38.)

**Busy, Buzzy Bee/
Say It Slowly, Say It Quickly**

40

Specific Skills: Phonemic Awareness

Segmenting Phonemes

When children can demonstrate the skill of blending isolated phonemes to create words, have them listen to words and then separate the sounds in those words. This skill is the reverse of blending phonemes. For example, if you say cub, have children repeat the sounds quickly until the word cub can be heard. Tailor the lessons by determining how many phonemes the children will blend. For those children in kindergarten, select words that have two or three phonemes. Older students are capable of handling words with up to four phonemes if blends and digraphs have been explained to them

Banking On Sounds

Each student will need a copy of the Banking on Sounds "piggy bank" pattern found on page 42 and at least 10 pennies. Using real pennies can be a lot of fun, but if this is not possible, make copies of the penny patterns at the bottom of the page.

The teacher should generate words from classroom materials or from a favorite children's book. The teacher says a word and then the children place a penny for each phoneme heard in the piggy bank.

Climbing the Phoneme Ladder Game

Have the students work in teams of four. Each team will need a copy of the "Climbing the Phoneme Ladder" game board found on pages 44–45. Each team can make their own game board by coloring it and then taping the two pages together. For added durability, the game board can be glued to the inside of a file folder. Each student will also need a game marker (i.e., math counter, coin, eraser). For each team, copy and cut out two sets of the game cards found on page 43.

Have the students sit with their teammates and as a class, look at each card, say the name of the picture, and decide how many phonemes are in each word. Write that number on the back of each game card. This is good preparation for the teams to play the game independently.

Now, everyone is ready to play the game and should place their game markers on the "start" space. Place the cards on the card pile space on the game board with the picture face up (the written number face down). Next, the players take turns drawing cards. Once a card is drawn the player says the name of the picture and how many phonemes are in that word. If the player is correct, the game marker is moved that same number of spaces on the game board as the number of phonemes in that word. For example, if the player says the word jet and says that jet has three phonemes /j/ /e/ /t/, that player would then move his game marker up the ladder three spaces. If the player is wrong, he is not allowed to move his game marker. The play then passes to the next person after either a right or wrong response. The first person to climb the ladder to the top of the tree house is the winner.

Team Up with Sound It Out Kids

Enlarge and copy onto colored card stock 18 "Sound It Out Kids" found on page 39. Copy the picture cards found on page 46, cut out, and glue the pictures onto the "kids" T-shirts. Keep two of the kids blank. Have the students listen to the sounds in CVC words. Students should find the corresponding Sound It Out Kid cutout that represents the initial and final consonant sound of the word, linking the cutouts together just like assembling a puzzle.

Banking On Sounds

Pictures: Row I: dog, fish, tub, car; Row 2: jar, box, book, drum; Row 3: rope, cheese, chair, peach; Row 4: pig, coat, key, kite; Row 5: cow, star, jet, slide

Climbing the Phoneme Ladder Game Cards

(Directions are found on page 41.)

Climbing the Phoneme Ladder Game Board

Specific Skills: Phonemic Awareness

START

Pictures: Row I: bus, jug, mop, net;
Row 2: rug, tooth, fish, kite;
Row 3: web, sail, cat, dog;
Row 4: goat, hen, pig, leaf

Team Up with Sound It Out Kids Cards
(Directions are found on page 41.)

Recognizing Syllables

The realization that words are made up of units of sound called syllables is another important listening skill for young learners. This skill development can actually start when children are beginning to blend on-sets and rimes to make words. Larger units of sound can be easier to hear and identify then the individual phonemes in words.

Sing and Say Words with Two Beats

For a fun and easy way to introduce the concept of syllables, have children sing the following song and say simple compound words that have two beats. Children who are familiar with this song will quickly say the word to the beat of the music instead of clapping at the end of the sentence. Examples of compound words include *airplane, anthill, backdoor, backpack, backyard, bathtub,*  *beanbag, bedroom, bedtime, beehive, birdcage, birdhouse, birthday, bookmark, bulldog, classroom, corncob, doghouse, doorbell, downhill, football, goldfish, haircut, homework, mailbox, notebook, popcorn, rainbow, rooftop, sailboat, seagull, sidewalk, snowball, starfish, toenail,* and *upstairs.* Tell children what word to say or have them supply words to use when singing the song.

If You Know a Compound Word, Say It Now!
Sung to the tune of "If You're Happy"

If you know a compound word, say it now. [ex.: *cupcake*]
If you know a compound word, say it now. [ex.: *cupcake*]
If you're sure its a compound word, then your voice can say it loudly.
If you know a compound word, say it now. [ex.: *cupcake!*]

Syllable Shakers

To help children become familiar with the animals pictured on pages 50-54, make enlarged copies of the game boards on colorful cardstock and then cut out the individual pictures along the solid lines and for use as the playing cards. Use a clean yogurt container or margarine tub with lid and fill it partway with dried split green peas or rice to make a noisemaker. Secure the lid with duct tape or shipping tape. Print the numbers 1–4 individually on pieces of cardstock. Work with a small group of children. Place the game cards in a pile in the center of the playing area. Arrange the number cards in order as categories for sorting animal names by number of syllables. Have children take turns drawing a card, saying the name of the animal, and then repeating the name while shaking the container once for each syllable. Have the other players count the shakes and tell you their answers. Then, place the picture in the correct number category. Continue in this manner as time and interest allow.

Alternatively, after reading aloud a picture book, select words from the text that have two or more syllables. Choose children to tell you how many beats (syllables) they hear when you say the words. To help them hear the syllables, have children use shakers when pronouncing the words.

How Many Syllables? Game

To the Teacher: Copy the cards below onto colorful cardstock to give each child a set of numbers 1–4. Cut out the cards along the dashed lines. Glue each card onto a craft stick.

To play the game, read each word aloud slowly, segmenting it into syllables. Have children hold up their corresponding card for the number of syllables in the word. Continue the game as time and interest allow.

1. but-ter-fly
2. rob-in
3. el-e-phant
4. ti-ger
5. mon-key
6. whale
7. al-i-ga-tor
8. fish
9. pup-py
10. cat-er-pil-lar
11. lamp
12. car-pet
13. cab-i-net
14. ta-ble
15. pi-an-o
16. sal-a-man-der
17. ov-en
18. mi-cro-wave
19. bowl
20. dish-es
21. chair
22. steps
23. cook-ie
24. di-no-saur

1	2	3	4
1	2	3	4
1	2	3	4

Roll and Match

Copy the die onto card stock and fold and glue according to the directions on the tabs. Next, copy the "Roll and Match" game boards found on pages 50–54.

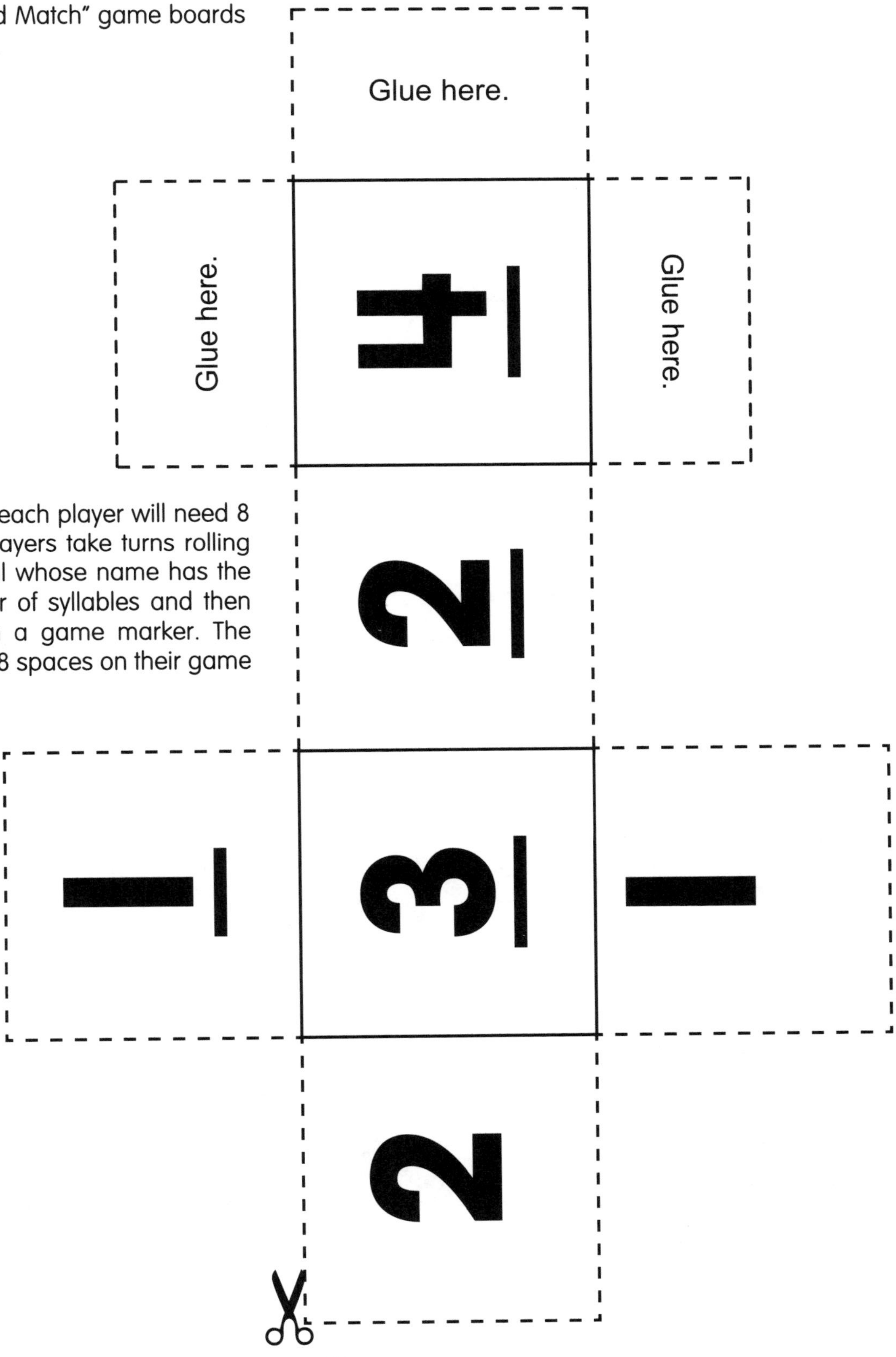

Glue here.

Glue here.

4

Glue here.

2

To play the game, each player will need 8 game markers. The players take turns rolling the die, find an animal whose name has the corresponding number of syllables and then cover that space with a game marker. The first player to cover all 8 spaces on their game board is the winner.

1

3

1

2

(Roll and Match game cards are also used in the activity "Syllable Shakers." Directions are found on page 47.)

(Recognizing Syllables)

(Directions are found on page 49.)

Roll and Match

(Roll and Match game cards are also used in the activity "Syllable Shakers." Directions are found on page 47.)

(Recognizing Syllables)

(Directions are found on page 49.)

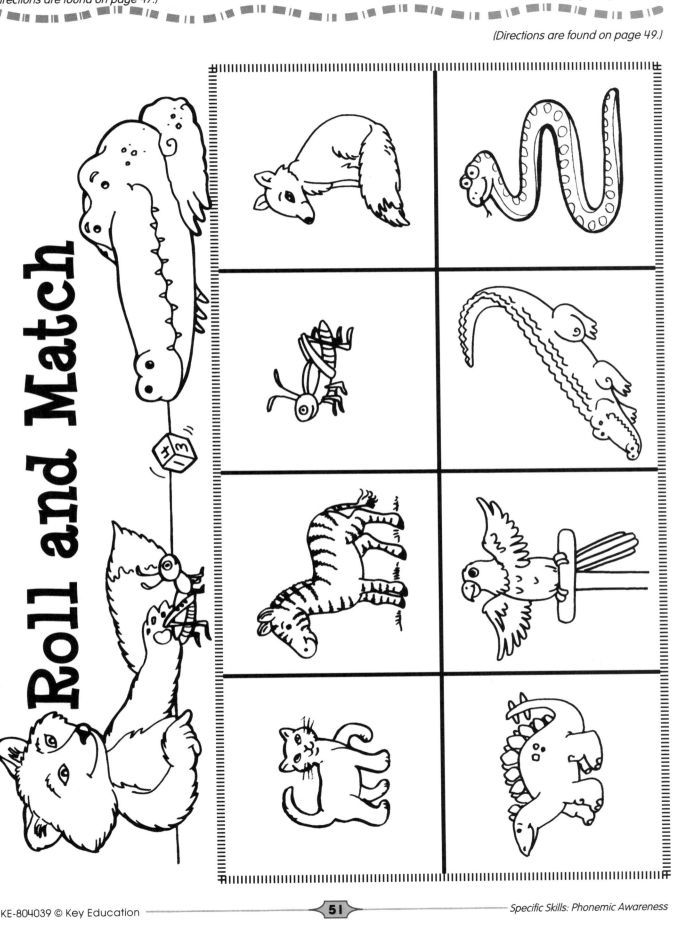

(Roll and Match game cards are also used in the activity "Syllable Shakers."
Directions are found on page 47.)

(Recognizing Syllables)

(Directions are found on page 49.)

(Roll and Match game cards are also used in the activity "Syllable Shakers." Directions are found on page 47.)

(Recognizing Syllables)

(Directions are found on page 49.)

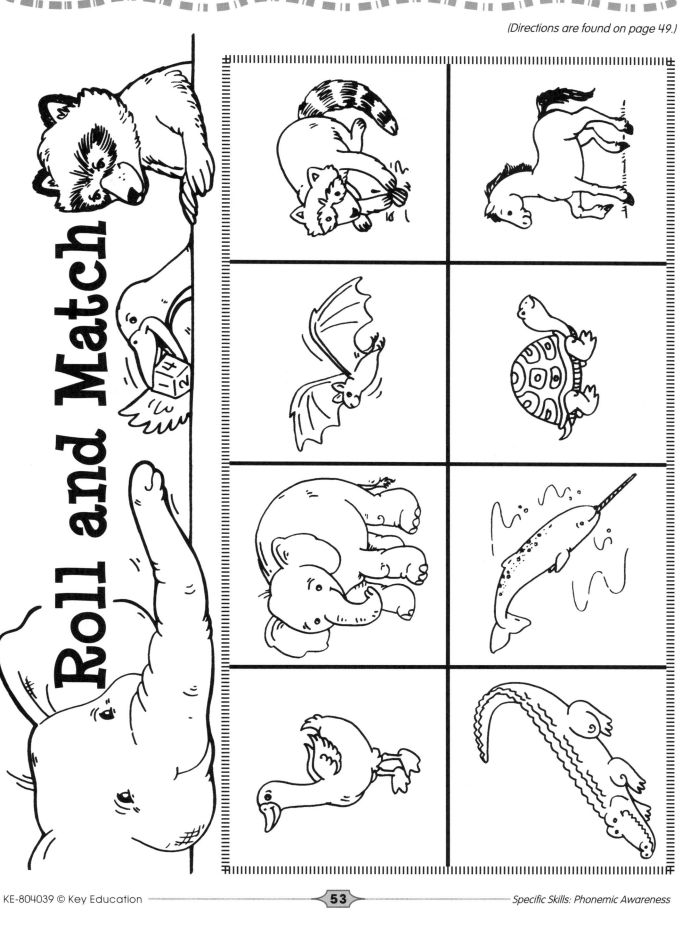

(Roll and Match game cards are also used in the activity "Syllable Shakers." Directions are found on page 47.)

(Recognizing Syllables)

(Directions are found on page 49.)

Roll and Match

Counting Syllables

To the Teacher: Have children practice identifying the syllables in spoken words by clapping. Say the names of the pictures aloud. Have children repeat the names and clap for each syllable. Then, direct them to circle the numeral that corresponds with the number of syllables in the word.

Counting Syllables—A

	1	2	3	4
	1	2	3	4
	1	2	3	4
	1	2	3	4

To the Teacher: Name the picture. Have children circle the numeral that corresponds with the number of syllables in the word.

Counting Syllables—B

	1	2	3	4
	1	2	3	4
	1	2	3	4
	1	2	3	4

To the Teacher: Name the picture. Have children circle the numeral that corresponds with the number of syllables in the word.

Manipulating Phonemes

The most difficult skills when changing individual sounds in spoken words are to substitute, add, and delete phonemes to build new words. Only after children have had rich experiences with rhyming words, recognizing alliterative phrases, isolating sounds, and blending phonemes would it be appropriate for them to apply these new skills in word-play game and lessons. The following examples explain further how to use these advance phonemic awareness skills:

Phoneme and Sound Unit Substitution

To practice this skill, first have the children answer word riddles using onset (initial consonants) and rimes. Then, proceed to riddles that incorporate initial blends and digraphs as onsets. For example: What word begins with /m/ and rhymes with *top*? What word begins with /dr/ and rhymes with *top*? What word begins with /ch/ and rhymes with *top*?

Phoneme Deletion

When children can easily hear and count individual phonemes in words, then they are ready to try deleting sounds to make new words. For example: Take away the /f/ sound in the word *flock*. What is the new word? (*lock*) Take away the /t/ sound in the word *train*. What is the new word? (*rain*) The answers do not always have to be actual words. For additional practice, have children answer riddles like these: What word would be left if you take away the /k/ sound in *snack*? (*sna*) Take away the /s/ sound in *snack*. (*nack*) Another example would be: Take away the /p/ sound in *clamp*. (*clam*) Take away the /k/ sound in *clamp*. (*lamp*) Take away the /l/ sound in *clamp*. (*camp*)

Phoneme Addition

For this skill, generate riddles that ask children to add certain sounds to chosen phonograms or words. This type of exercise is also an effective way to introduce a read-aloud book that incorporates wonderful language play in its title. Check on your bookshelf for potential activity ideas. For example, before reading aloud the book *Smash! Mash! Crash! There Goes the Trash!* by Barbara Odanaka, think of word riddles for the -*ash* family. Examples include the following: What word rhymes with *ash* and begins with /b/? (*bash*) Begins with /d/? (*dash*) Begins with /l/? (*lash*) What word rhymes with *lash* and begins with /f/? (*flash*) Begins with /s/? (*slash*) Begins with /k/? (*clash*) What word rhymes with *mash* and begins with /s/? (*smash*) What word rhymes with *rash* and begins with /tr/? (*trash*) Begins with /kr/? (*crash*) After this fun word play activity, everyone is ready to read more about trash!

Sample Read-Aloud Books

No doubt, there are wonderful picture books with delightful language play on your book shelf. Try to locate titles with playful storylines, rhyming patterns, or strings of nonsense words that draw attention to sounds.
- *The Cow that Went OINK* by Bernard Most (Harcourt Brace Jovanovich, 1990)
- *Rub-a-Dub Sub* by Linda Ashman (Harcourt Brace Jovanovich, 2003)
- *Rattletrap Car* by Phyllis Root (Candlewick Press, 2001)
- Dr. Seuss titles—choose your favorites!

Phoneme Manipulation

Copy pages 58–60 onto card stock, color, and cut out. Each card has two pictures representing either a phoneme addition, phoneme deletion, or phoneme substitution. For example, when adding a /t/ to *rain*, the new word is *train* (phoneme addition). When deleting the /s/ in *skid* the new word is *kid*. When substituting the /c/ in *cake* for /r/ the new word is *rake*.

Variation 1: Using a large piece of paper with three different headings (+, –, and s) students can place each card under the appropriate headings. For example, the card with *ice* and *rice* would do under the "+" column.

Variation 2: The cards can also be used as teaching tools. The teacher can sort the cards by skill. For example, if phoneme addition is the skill being practiced, the teacher could then fold the card in two and say the name of the first picture, such as *ear*. Then, ask the child what the word would be if /t/ was added to the word *ear (tear)*.

Pictures: Row I: rain/train, lap/clap; Row 2: ear/tear, ice/rice; Row 3: lid/slid, lock/clock

(Directions are found on page 58.)

Pictures: Row 1: top/stop, blast/last; Row 2: nail/snail, candy/Andy; Row 3: turkey/key, skid/kid;
Row 4: ring/wing, bone/phone

(Directions are found on page 58.)

Pictures: Row 1: goat/boat, cake/rake; Row 2: cat/rat, hen/pen; Row 3: dice/mice, cot/dot;
Row 4: house/mouse, dog/frog

60

Specific Skills: Phonemic Awareness

Spin for Sounds—Letter Wheel A

To the Teacher: Copy the wheel below onto colorful cardstock and then cut it out. Using a commercial metal spinner, attach it to the middle of the wheel using a brad. Have children take turns spinning the arrow. When the arrow lands on a consonant, call out a word family (rime) for the player. Have the child say the sound for the letter shown on the dial (onset) and then combine it with the rime to make a word that could be real or nonsense.

Word Families: -at, -et, -ill, -oo, -ub

Spin for Sounds—Letter Wheel B

To the Teacher: Copy the wheel below onto colorful cardstock and then cut it out. Using a commercial metal spinner, attach it to the middle of the wheel using a brad. Have children take turns spinning the arrow. When the arrow lands on a consonant, call out a word family (rime) for the player. Have the child say the sound for the letter shown on the dial (onset) and then combine it with the rime to make a word that could be real or nonsense.

Word Families: -ay -ed, -ip, -ot, -ut

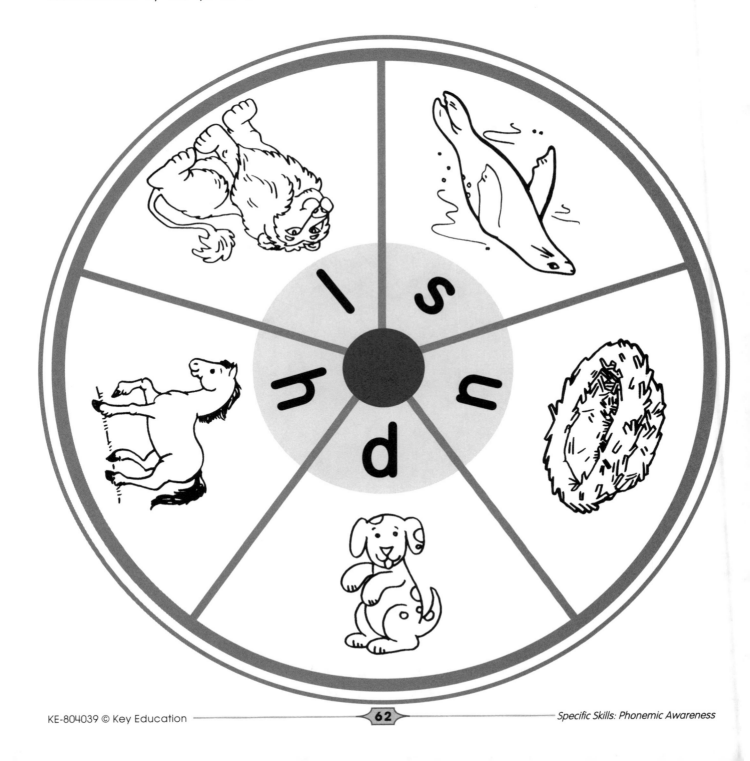

WEBSITES

Big Ideas in Beginning Reading
http://reading/uoregon.edu/pa/
This web site contains the answers to questions on beginning phonemic awareness asked by teachers or by those who seek to expand their knowledge.

Phonemic Awareness Activities for the Classroom: Resources for K–3 Teachers
http://www.k-3learningpages.net/web%20phonemic%20awareness.htm
This web site provides a variety of innovative and detailed ideas that teachers can implement into their lesson plans in regard to helping students develop phonemic awareness. In addition, this web site contains guidelines that teachers can adhere to when teaching phonemic awareness.

Phonemic Awareness Activities
http://www.sasked.gov.sk.ca/docs/ela/e_literacy/awareness.html
This web site includes several excellent phonemic awareness activities and gives examples of the activities. The web site includes a main menu that provides access to many early literacy tools and documents.

Phonemic Awareness, Alphabetics, and Sight Words
http://www.readingtarget.com/Basics.htm
This web site lists different activities that teach Phonemic Awareness and Alphabetics. There are also links a teacher can click on which will take them to Phonics Grades 1, 2, and 3. Each grade level displays a list of phonics tests and lessons that can be used.

Phonemic Awareness for Young Language Learners
http://www.esl4kids.net/phonics.html
This website has many different activities for teachers to use for phonemic awareness. It gives the actual example of an activity and also includes such information as the objective of the activity, group size to be used, prep time, playing time, interest level, and ability level.

ProTeacher-Phonemic Awareness
http://www.proteacher.com/070171.shtml
On this website, you will find a vast range of topics that deal with phonemic awareness, and there are numerous excellent ideas provided for lesson plans. Some lessons include games that focus on rhyming skills, how to teach children to break up and identify the sounds found in words, and word hunts in which students look for specific sounds or patterns in a story they are familiar with. Included on this website are extensive links to websites that address classroom issues for teachers when teaching phonemic awareness.

Reading Strategy #4: Phonemic Awareness
http://dragonnet.hkis.edu.hk/lp/learningcenter/RS4.htm
This fantastic web site begins by explaining Phonemic Awareness. The web site also lists activities that include playing rhyming games, and that use physical responses such as clapping and tapping to demonstrate patterns in songs, stories, and words.

Standards Correlation

This book supports the NCTE/IRA Standards for the English Language Arts and the recommended teaching practices outlined in the NAEYC/IRA position statement Learning to Read and Write: Developmentally Appropriate Practices for Young Children.

──────────── NCTE/IRA Standards for the English Language Arts ────────────

Each activity in this book supports one or more of the following standards:

1. **Students read many different types of print and nonprint texts for a variety of purposes.** Children must read a variety of pictures in order to do the activities and play the games in *Phonemic Awareness.*

2. **Students read literature from various time periods, cultures, and genres in order to form an understanding of humanity.** Each section of *Phonemic Awareness* includes literature suggestions for teachers to use as read-alouds and for teachers to place in their classroom libraries for students to read on their own.

3. **Students use a variety of strategies to build meaning while reading.** *Phonemic Awareness* promotes the development of a wide range of phonemic awareness skills and strategies, including matching initial sounds in words; isolating phonemes; and blending, segmenting, and manipulating phonemes. In addition, several of the activities strengthen awareness of environmental sounds and rhyming words and build syllable recognition and classification skills.

4. **Students communicate in spoken, written, and visual form, for a variety of purposes and a variety of audiences.** Throughout *Phonemic Awareness,* students communicate verbally through chanting rhymes and playing word games and visually through gestures and drawings.

5. **Students become participating members of a variety of literacy communities.** *Phonemic Awareness* contains many group games that help teachers build literacy communities.

──── NAEYC/IRA Position Statement Learning to Read and Write: Developmentally Appropriate Practices for Young Children ────

Each activity in this book supports one or more of the following recommended teaching practices for preschool students:

1. **Adults create positive relationships with children by talking with them, modeling reading and writing, and building children's interest in reading and writing.** The read-aloud suggestions, games, and activities in *Phonemic Awareness* all encourage teachers to model reading behavior for their students, effectively building students' interest in reading.

2. **Teachers read to children daily, both as individuals and in small groups. They select high-quality, culturally diverse reading materials.** Each section of *Phonemic Awareness* contains read-aloud suggestions, and many of the activities in it contain a read-aloud component.

3. **Teachers provide opportunities for children to discuss what has been read to them, focusing on both language structure and content.** Several of the activities in *Phonemic Awareness* have students talk about the rhyming words in the books their teacher has read to them.

4. **Teachers promote the development of phonemic awareness through appropriate songs, finger plays, games, poems, and stories.** *Phonemic Awareness* focuses particularly on teaching a wide range of phonemic awareness skills, so it contains many games, rhymes, and activities that support this standard.

5. **Teachers provide experiences and materials that help children expand their vocabularies.** *Phonemic Awareness* presents many pictures and words that help build students' vocabularies.

Each activity in this book supports one or more of the following recommended teaching practices for kindergarten and primary-grade students:

1. **Teachers read to children daily and provide opportunities for students to read independently both fiction and nonfiction texts.** Each section of *Phonemic Awareness* contains read-aloud suggestions, and many of the activities in it contain a read-aloud component. In addition, teachers are encouraged to add books that support phonemic awareness to their classroom libraries so that students can look at them independently.

2. **Teachers provide balanced literacy instruction that incorporates systematic phonics instruction along with meaningful reading and writing activities.** This book contains phonemic awareness activities that build a necessary foundation for phonics instruction.

3. **Teachers provide opportunities for children to work in small groups.** *Phonemic Awareness* includes many small group games and activities.

4. **Teachers provide challenging instruction that expands children's knowledge of their world and expands their vocabularies.** *Phonemic Awareness* presents many pictures and words that help build students' vocabularies.

Daily Book Scanning Log

Name: Ronailyn Tablante
Greisy manzo

Date: 11/05/2024   # of Scanners: 2

BIN #	BOOKS COMPLETED	# OF PAGES	NOTES / EXCEPTIONS
Bin 1	37	7262	
Bin 2			
Bin 3			
Bin 4			
Bin 5			
Bin 6			
Bin 7			
Bin 8			
Bin 9			
Bin 10			
Bin 11			
Bin 12			
Bin 13			
Bin 14			
Bin 15			
Bin 16			
Bin 17			
Bin 18			
Bin 19			
Bin 20			
Bin 21			
Bin 22			
Bin 23			
Bin 24			
Bin 25			
Bin 26			
Bin 27			
Bin 28			
Bin 29			
Bin 30			
Bin 31			
Bin 32			
Bin 33			
Bin 34			
Bin 35			
Bin 36			
Bin 37			
Bin 38			
Bin 39			
Bin 40			

(BOOKS / LIBROS) TOTAL: _____ / 600

(PAGES/PAGINAS) TOTAL: _____

SHIFT: 1   STATION #: 15